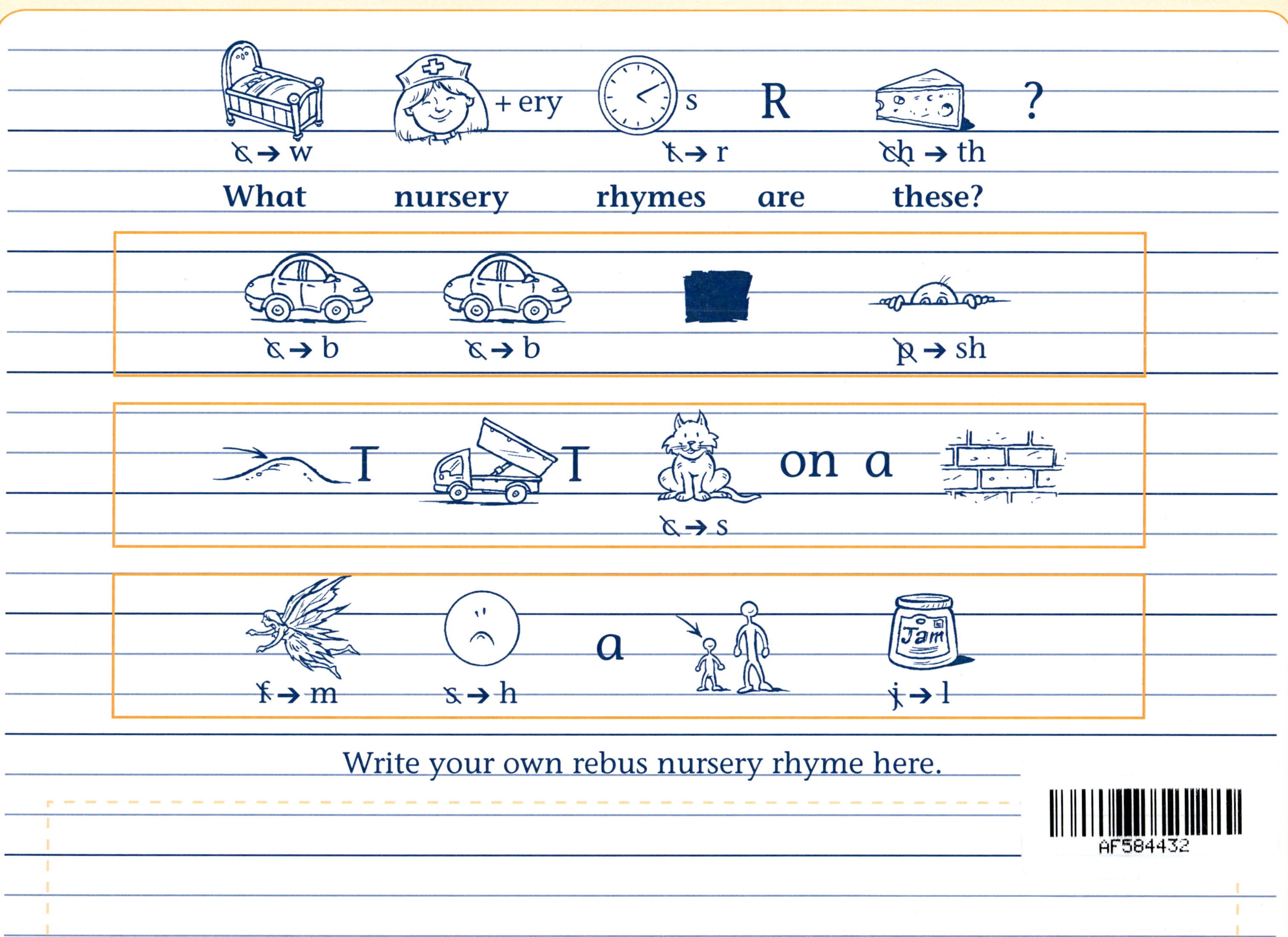
c → w
+ ery
s
t → r
R
ch → th
?
What nursery rhymes are these?
c → b
c → b
p → sh
T
T
c → s
on a
f → m
s → h
a
Jam
j → l
Write your own rebus nursery rhyme here.

Contents and curriculum links

Page number		Content	Eng Language	Eng Literature	Eng Literacy	History	Maths	Science	Other
1		Rebus nursery rhymes		•	•				
2		Contents and curriculum links			•				
3		Getting ready to write	•		•				
4		Concepts of writing	•		•				
5		Purpose of writing	•		•				
6		Letter formation: Cursive style	•		•				
7		Instructions: Anti-clockwise letter formation	•		•				
8		Instructions: Clockwise letter formation	•		•				
9		Instructions: Downward letter formation – i family	•		•				
10		Instructions: Downward letter formation – u family	•		•				
11		Reference: Starting point and direction	•		•				
12	a	Things with arms	•		•				
13	b	Car parts	•		•				
14	c	*Lunch munch* rhyme		•	•				
15	Fl.	*Lots of Socks* poem		•	•				
16	d	Ordinal numbers			•		•		
17	e	Ways to eat eggs			•				H & P E
18	f	Marine signal flags	•		•	•			
19	Fl.	Recipe	•		•				
20	g	Birds and their young			•			•	
21	h	Honey bees			•			•	
22	i	Word play	•		•				
23	j	Jigsaws			•			•	Tech
24	Fl.	Rhyming pairs	•		•				
25	k	Australian birds			•			•	
26	l	*Yum! Salad!* poem		•	•				
27	m	Machines			•			•	Tech
28	n	Australian animals	•		•			•	
29	Fl.	Practising numbers			•		•		
30	o	Opposites	•		•		•		
31	p	Word-building	•		•				
32	WYO	Compound words	•		•				
33	q	Word meanings	•		•				
34	r	*Gingerbread Man* refrain		•	•				
35	Fl. Nos	Numbers and patterns			•		•		
36	s	The sun			•			•	
37	t	Hard-shelled reptiles			•			•	
38	u	Riddle	•		•				
39	WYO	Signs	•		•				
40	v	Odd and even numbers			•		•		
41	WYO	Games or sports			•				H & P E
42	w	*Winter* poem		•	•				
43	WYO	An ideal tree house			•				
44	x	Counting-out rhyme	•		•				
45	y	Riddles	•		•				
46	z	Word play	•		•				
47	WYO	A bird story			•				
48		End of year assessment			•				

Fl. = Fluency page WYO = Write Your Own page

1 Hold your pencil like this.
Hold it **lightly** so your h and doesn't get tired.

2 Sit facing your desk, or turn slightly.
Turn your paper also.

Right-handers sit like this.

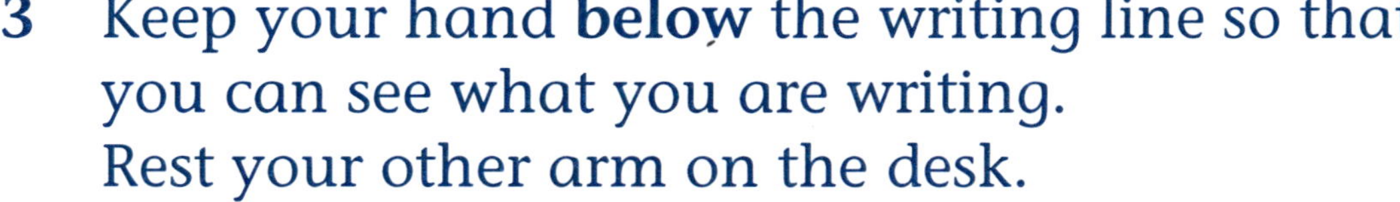

3 Keep your hand **below** the writing line so that you can see what you are writing.
Rest your other arm on the desk.

Try not to write across your body. Keep the paper on the side of your body that you write with.

Left-handers sit like this.

Concepts of writing

Writing is made up of letters and words.

Letters e g k n s t w

Words pet friend dog

Sentences I love my cat.

Her name is Tiger.

Letters make different sounds in different words.

Spaces between the words make the writing easier to read.

A sentence is a group of words that makes a whole thought or idea.

Purpose of writing

Writing is very useful. It is also good fun.

You can

tell stories

describe what you see

write messages

label things

make lists

and have fun with
words and ideas.

1 Most letters start at the **top** and have strong **down strokes.**

h j o u

2 Most letters have **crisp turns**. This makes a **wedge** shape inside many letters.

b e a h

3 Many letters have **exits** and some have **entries**. This makes it easier to do joined writing later on.

d m r t

4 The writing has a slight **slope** to help with fluency. You may write straight up and down if you prefer.

car wish

5 All letters have a **body**. Some also have a **head** or a **tail**. The letter **f** has all three!

c i n s u f

d k l t p y

Anti-clockwise letters: a c g q d e o f s

a c g q

Start at the top (1 o'clock).
Move anti-clockwise.
Finish letters **a** and **q** with an exit.

d e

Start in the middle.
Move anti-clockwise.
Finish with an exit.

o f s

Start at the top.
Move anti-clockwise.
Letter **o** has an exit.
Letter **f** has a tail and two strokes.

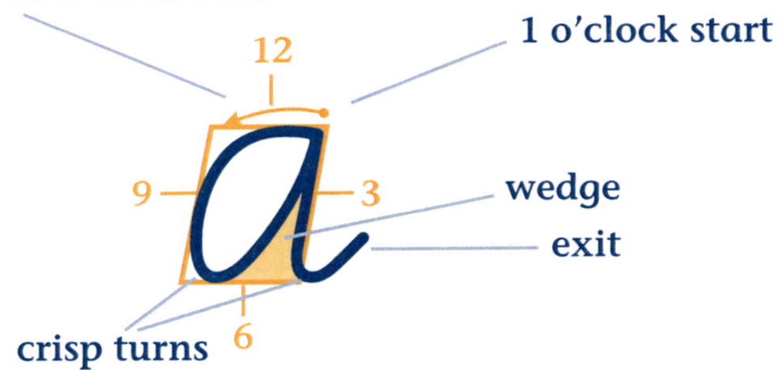

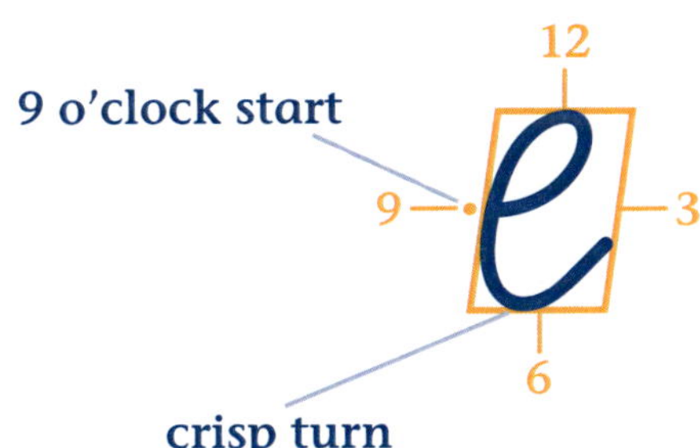

Instructions: Clockwise letter formation

Clockwise letters: m n r x z   h k p

m n r	Start with a small entry. Move down, then clockwise. Finish with an exit.
x z	Start with a small entry. Move clockwise. Letter **x** has two strokes. Letter **z** has a flattened tail.
h k p	Start at the top. Move down, then clockwise. Finish with an exit.

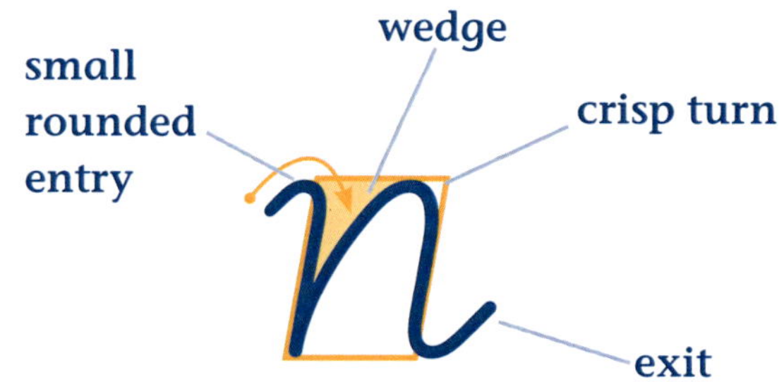

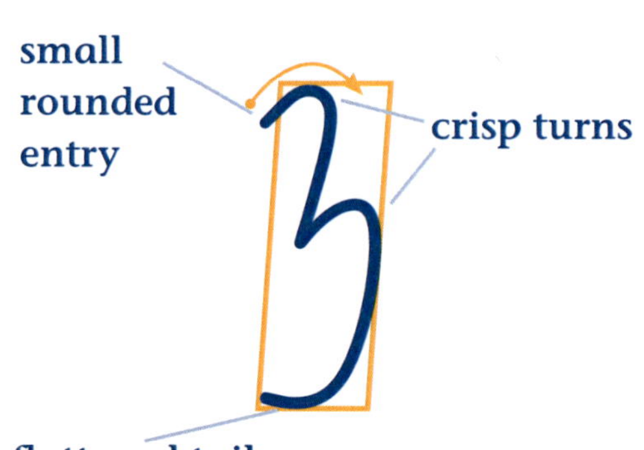

Downward letters: the *i* family i l t j

i l t

Start at the top.
Move ↓ downwards.
Finish with an exit.
Letter **t** has two strokes.

j

Start at the top.
Move ↓ downwards.
Finish with a flattened tail.

First stroke finishes with exit.

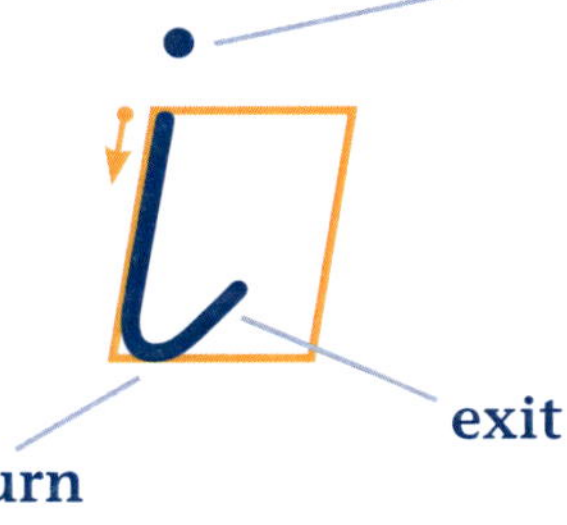

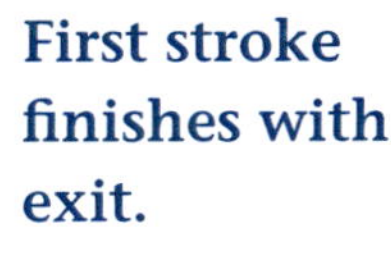

First stroke finishes with exit.

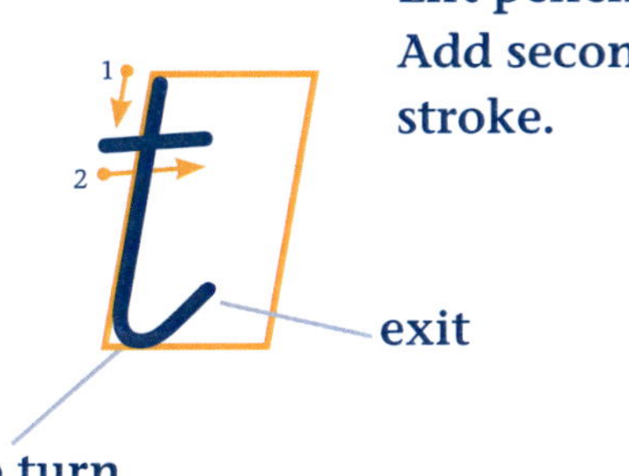

Instructions: Downward letter formation – u family

Downward letters: the *u* family u v w b y

u v w b

Start at the top.
Move ↓ downwards.
Finish with an exit.

y

Start at the top.
Move ↓ downwards.
Finish with a flattened tail.

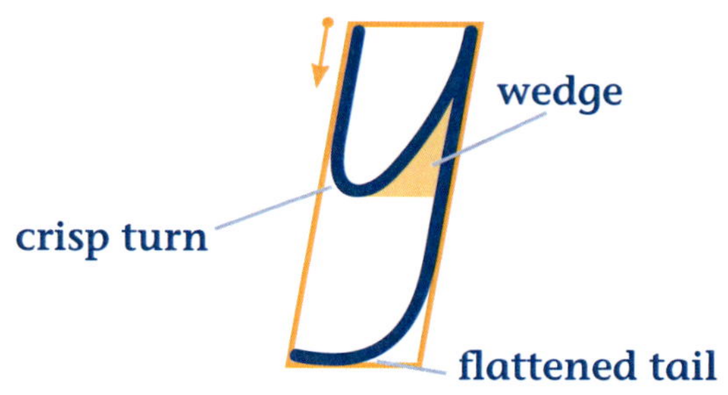

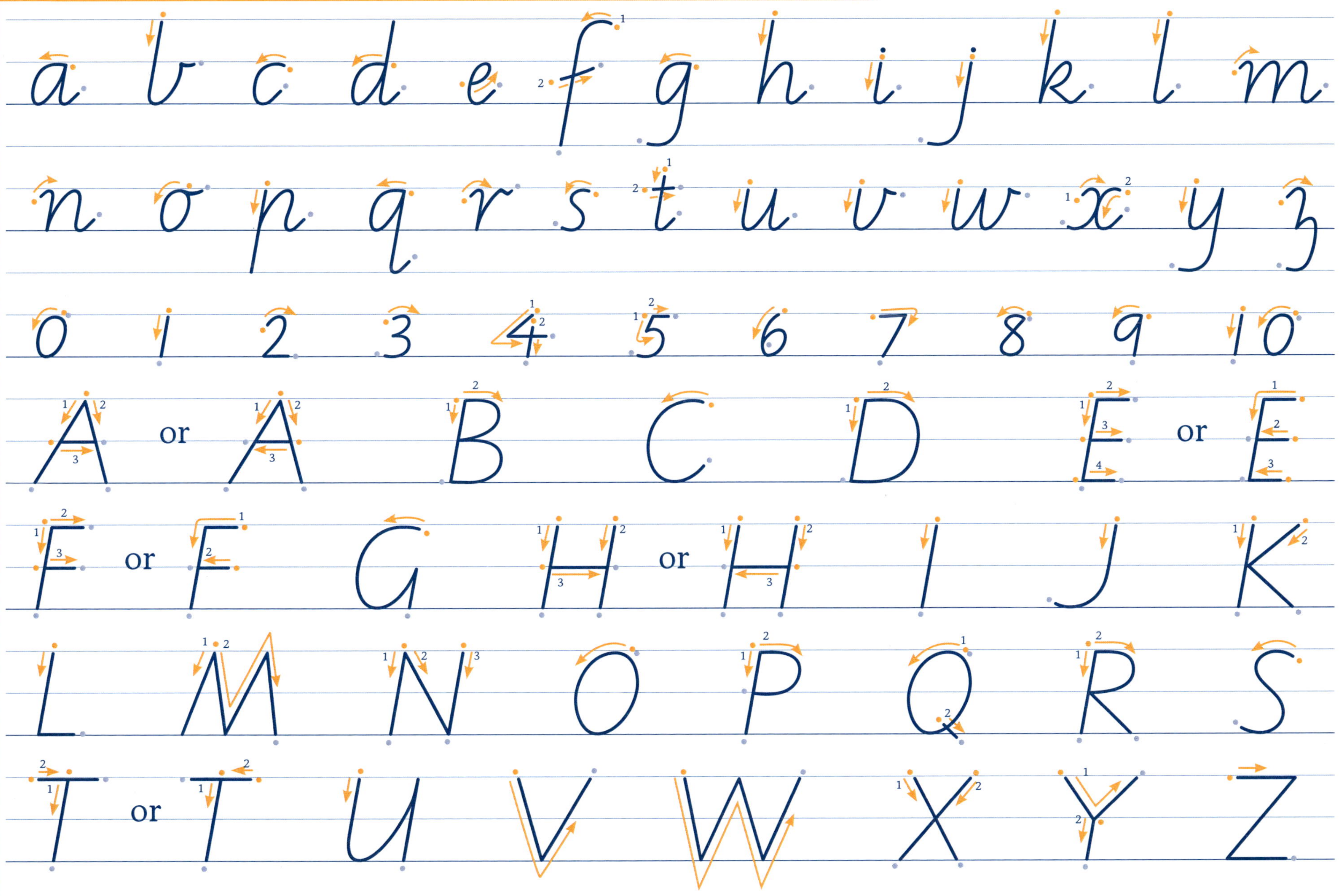

• starting point ↓ direction • finishing point

UPPER CASE: alternative formations are for left-handers.

Humans have arms.

Armchairs have arms.

Seastars have arms.

ll ll b b b B B

Brakes slow the car down.

The boot is at the back.

The bonnet is a lid.

Self-assess

Tick tock one o'clock

Time for lunch.

Munch munch crunch.

Spotty socks plain socks

White ones for sport.

Stripy socks bed socks

Long ones and short.

b b b d d d D D

Dina won.

Dave came second.

Their dog came third.

   e e e E E

Eggs are good to eat.

People eat them boiled,

fried or scrambled.

f f f F F

Flags are used on ships.

These flags spell FLAG.

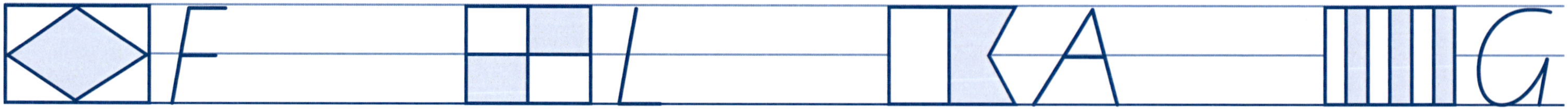

F L A G

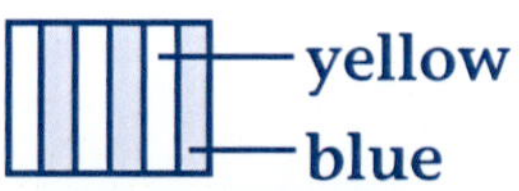

red
white

Fruity Ice Blocks

1 Measure 200 mL of juice.

2 Pour into an ice-cube tray.

3 Freeze overnight. 4 Enjoy!

g g g
G G
goose
gosling
eagle
eaglet
swan
cygnet

h h h H H

Honey bees collect nectar from flowers. They make it into honey in their hives.

Self-assess

||| ||| ||| i i i l l

I scream for ice-cream:

vanilla chocolate chip

lime licorice apricot

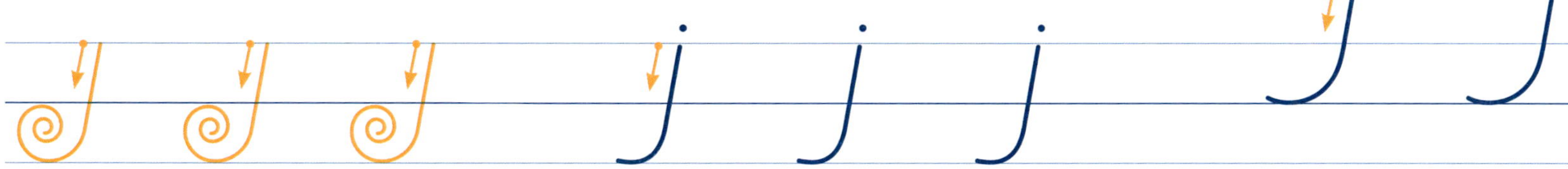

Jig saws cut curves.

Jigsaws have curved pieces.

Jig saws cut jigsaws.

egg riddle → yolk joke

catch a taxi → grab a

joking rabbit → funny

quick game → short

hawk

kookaburra

duck

kingfisher

cockatoo

kestrel

Self-assess

/// /// ///   l l l   L L

Yum! Lovely lettuce salad.

Delicious noodle salad.

Luscious coleslaw.

m m m m m M M

Machines can mow 

mix  measure 

make 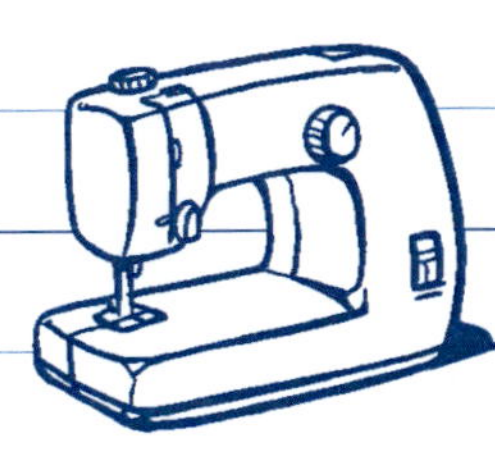 and move. 

n n n N N

Some Australian animals:

goanna bandicoot

echidna kangaroo

1 2 3 4 5 6 7 8 9 10

2 4 6 8 10 12 14 16

5 10 15 20 25 30 35 40 45 50

3 4 5 6 7 8

Opposites: in and out

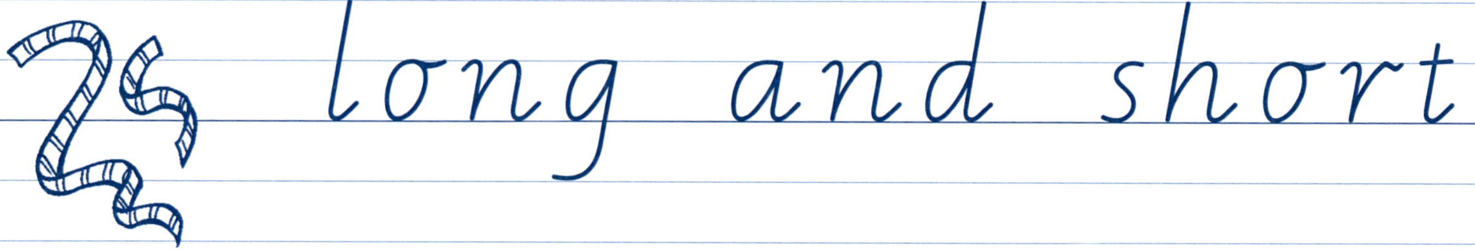

long and short

above and below

Start with a pine tree.

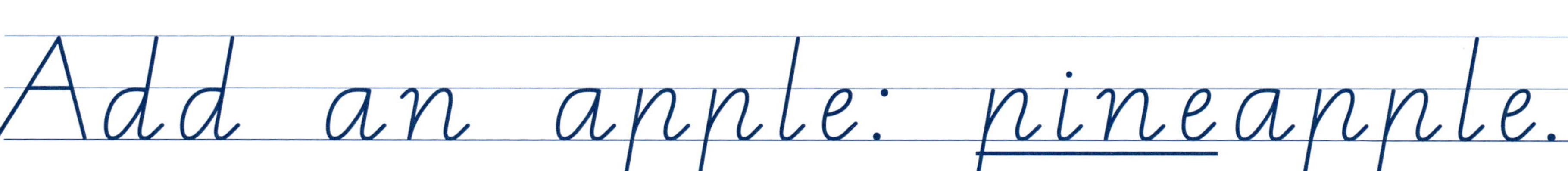

Add an apple: pineapple.

Or put s in front: spine.

Self-assess

Write the word for each picture.

el

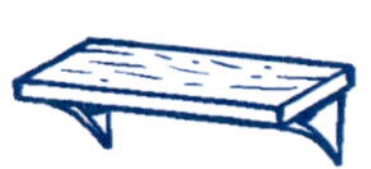

Write the compound word for each picture.

Quads: 4 babies born together

Squad: a group of people working as a team

r r r R R

Run, run, as fast as you can,

you can't catch me,

I'm the gingerbread man.

How many?	What's the total?	What's the pattern?
	6 + 3 =	3 6 9 15
	8 + 9 =	7 17 37 47
	5 + 5 + 5 =	62 61 60 58
	40 + 12 =	2 4 8 32

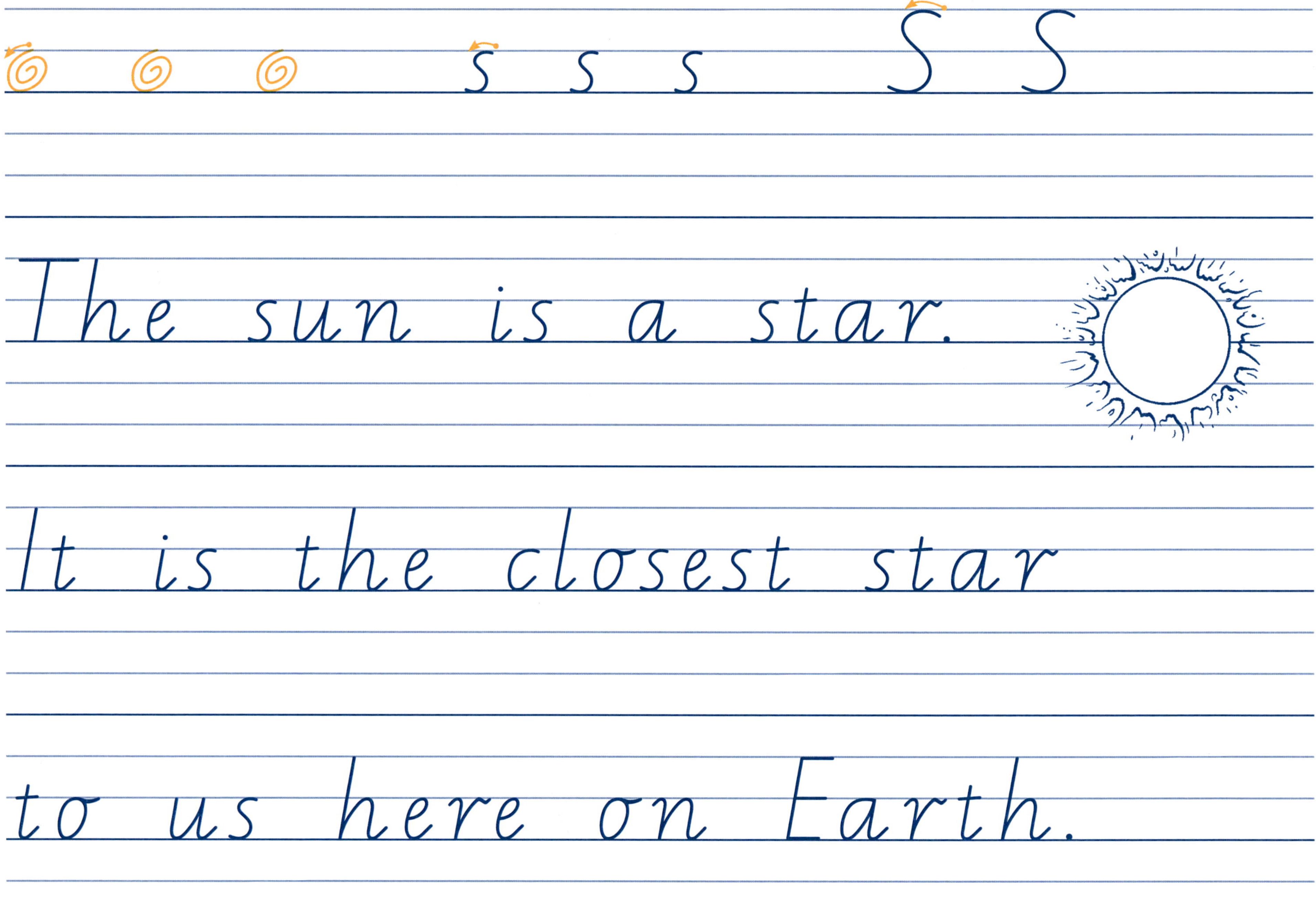
s s s
S S
The sun is a star.
It is the closest star
to us here on Earth.

t t t T T

Hard-shelled reptiles

Tortoises live on land.

Turtles live in the sea.

U U U u u u U U

Q: Why did the sultana

go out with the prune?

A: It couldn't find a date!

Write your own: Signs

Sign	Where can you see it?	What does it tell you?
 STOP		

 STATION ST		

v v v v v v V V

Five seven and eleven

are all odd numbers.

Twelve is an even number.

What do you like to play? Write about a game or sport that you enjoy. It could be a real game or a made-up one.

I play

I like it because

One day I

w w w w w W W

Wild winter weather,

Windy and wet.

In some places it snows.

Write your own: An ideal tree house

Imagine! You can have any tree house you want.
In any tree, with anything in it, as big (or small) as you like.

Write about your ideal tree house.

- What will it look like?
- How will you get into it?
- What will you do once you get there?

Self-assess

ɔɔ ɔɔ x x x X X

Six foxes playing.

Silver top taxi 1–2–3,

Silver top taxi, you're not he.

y y y y y y Y Y

Why is the letter E lazy?

Because it's always in bed.

Spell eighty in 2 letters: a–t

Self-assess

z z z ʒ ʒ ʒ Z Z

Fuzzy-wuzzy was a bear.

Fuzzy-wuzzy had no hair.

So he wasn't fuzzy was he?

Write you own: A bird story

Write a story about some of these birds. Their names are on pages 20 and 25.

Self-assess

I can write in CAPITALS

and in lower case too.

It's fun to write stories

made up or true.